IT'S ALL ABOUT THE SNACKS

Adventures in Petsitting

ALLISON NIVER

Charleston, SC
www.PalmettoPublishing.com

It's All About the Snacks
Adventures in petsitting

First Edition

Paperback: 979-8-88590-451-3

INTRODUCTION

Being among animals has always made me happy and satisfied with life. Now being an owner of a professional petsitting business, it gives me a daily dose of many types of creatures to enjoy and appreciate each day.

Little did I know it would also create a new passion for photography to combine with my love of animals.

Just like with humans, some are more photogenic than others. I apologize if one of your beloved is not included in this book; however, stay tuned. This may be #1 of many.

ENJOY

THANK YOU

First off, thanks to my friends for putting up with years of my crazy schedule. Also love to the past, present and future animals who continue to help me be who I am. To Palmetto Publishing- who put up with my lack of being tech savvy and helped make this dream of mine happen all from my very old Galaxy phone. And lastly, a huge thank you to my parents who instead of giving me a brother like I wanted, got me a dog. And as they say, the rest is history.

CHAPTER ONE

SONOMA LIVING
VINEYARD STYLE

CHAPTER TWO

LET'S GO FOR
A CAR RIDE

CHAPTER 3

LIFE ALWAYS INCLUDES PARTY HATS

AND ANOTHER KIND OF HAT

CHAPTER 4

WALKS WITH FRIENDS ARE THE BEST

CHAPTER 5

EVERYONE NEEDS
A BESTIE

CHAPTER 6

LIFE ON THE FARM

CHAPTER 7

TONGUES

CHAPTER 8

NOTHING LIKE SIBLING LOVE

CHAPTER 9

THINGS THAT CAN'T BE LEFT BEHIND

CHAPTER 10

JUST AWE...

THE END